REAL

OR

FAKE?

FAR-OUT FIBS, FISHY FACTS, AND PHONY PHOTOS TO TEST FOR THE TRUTH

LITTLE WHITE LIE

HONEST ABE

BIG OL' WHOPPER

EMILY KRIEGER
ILLUSTRATIONS BY TOM NICK COCOTOS

NATIONAL GEOGRAPHIC
WASHINGTON, D.C.

CONTENTS

Welcome to
REAL OR FAKE

How do you identify a lie? Sometimes it's hard to put your finger on a fake, but here are a few clues to help you along the way:

IT'S ALL IN THE DETAILS

Be on the lookout for details in a story that are inconsistent, or just seem impossible. Also, people have a tendency to over-explain when they're feeling guilty about something; likewise, some details in these stories just aren't necessary. Sometimes that can be a key identifier in figuring out where the truth is stretched.

USE YOUR NOGGIN'

If things in the story don't exactly line up with things you know to be true, go with what you know. Experience is one of the best teachers in life, so use yours when trying to determine what is real and what is fake.

GO WITH YOUR GUT

If things seem too unbelievable to be true, oftentimes they are. Trust your instincts when things seem off—a good rule for this book and in life!

LITTLE WHITE LIE

HONEST ABE

BIG OL' WHOPPER

WHAT'S A FIB-O-METER? A fib-o-meter is a handy little gauge we've invented for determining the level of a lie (or truth). The categories are: Honest Abe, Little White Lie, and Big Ol' Whopper. We've gone through and determined which story falls where based on whether it's true or how big a lie it is. If the story is true it falls in Honest Abe territory. If the details of the story are untrue and the lie is minor, we've gone with Little White Lie. If it was a big lie that maybe led to something else (widespread panic or disbelief, maybe), we've gone with Big Ol' Whopper. Agree with our findings? Decide for yourself as you rate things on the fib-o-meter!

AN OCTOPUS
THAT LIVES IN TREES

REAL OR FAKE?

The U.S. Pacific Northwest is wet—so wet that a sea creature lives in the region's trees! The Pacific Northwest tree octopus can be found swinging by its tentacles from the limbs of cedars and Douglas firs in the densely forested Olympic Peninsula, in Washington State. Cruising through the canopy like a chimp, it searches for insects and frogs to eat while keeping a watchful eye out for hawks and bald eagles. Dry summers are no problem for the octopus: It gets all the water it needs from the soggy moss draping the trees. A logger first reported the species to scientists in 1954. Before then, the wild, largely unexplored forests had kept the sea creature's existence a secret. Unfortunately, the removal of trees on the peninsula has drastically reduced the octopus's habitat, and it is now endangered. A website about the curious creature has been launched to help raise awareness and bring it back from the brink of extinction.

FAKE!

BIG OL'
WHOPPER

BUT PLENTY OF PEOPLE BELIEVE IN THE PACIFIC NORTHWEST TREE OCTOPUS.

Perhaps it's because of the widespread familiarity with the region's other mythical creature, Bigfoot. More likely the website, which is real, seems very convincing to some people. It includes such detailed information as "'Pacific Northwest Tree Octopus' is the correct popular name for *Octopus paxarbolis.* 'Pacific Northwestern Tree Octopus' is erroneous, much like using 'Canadian Geese' instead of 'Canada Geese.'"

FUN FACT

A 2007 study of average annual rainfall in 195 U.S. cities found that the Pacific Northwest ISN'T AS WET AS PEOPLE THINK IT IS. Not one city in the region cracked the top 10. Instead, the rainiest top 10 cities were all located in Florida, Alabama, Louisiana, and Texas.

HIGH SCHOOL
STOCK TRADER

High school students typically have long to-do lists: Go to class, do homework, finish chores, attend practice … trade stocks, make millions?! A self-taught financial whiz kid made headlines for earning millions from trading stocks—all before turning 18! The inspiring story of the New York City teenager appeared in magazines and newspapers, and *Business Insider* even put him on its annual "20 Under 20" list. The mini-money mogul bought himself a BMW—even though he didn't yet have a driver's license. He also rented a pricey Manhattan apartment—even though his parents wouldn't let him move out yet. While his fortune shocked many, his classmates reportedly weren't surprised: Everyone said that they knew he was a genius.

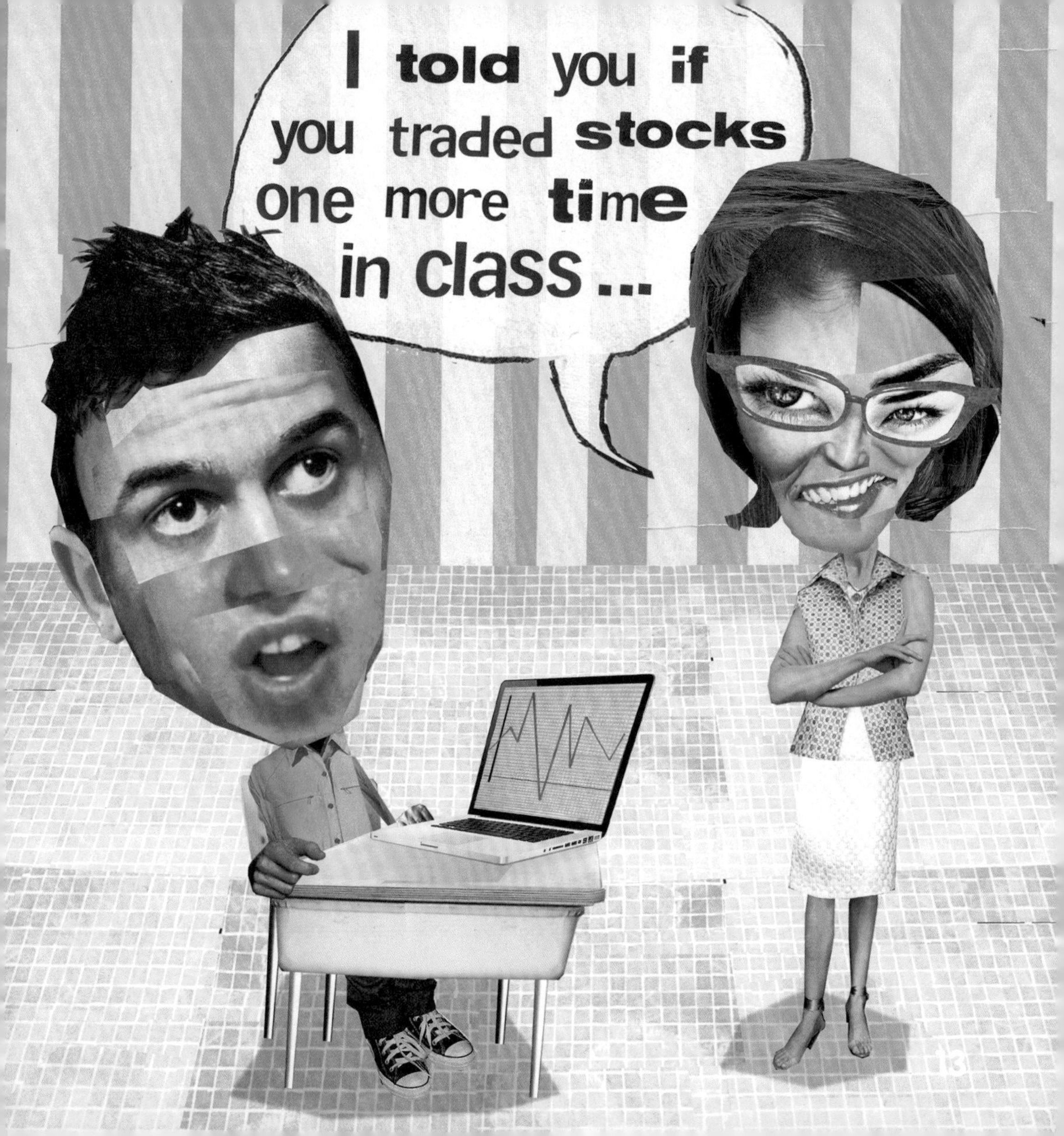
I told you if you traded stocks one more time in class ...

FAKE!

WHAT'S CRAZIER THAN A TEEN WHO TRADED STOCKS AND MADE MILLIONS?

A teen who made up a huge lie about making millions by trading stocks and managed to fool several major news outlets and countless people! As his story spread in 2013 and 2014, it eventually unraveled, and the teen finally admitted the whole thing was a lie. He did trade stocks, but they were simulated (not real) ones that he traded for his high school investment club.

FREAKY FACE
DISCOVERY

Scientists are reporting some news you might not want to hear: Tiny mites are crawling all over your parents' faces! The eight-legged critters were found to be living in the hair follicles of every single adult face tested during a study. Scientists were surprised, since previous tests showed that, at most, only half of adults have the creepy-crawlies on their faces. The amount and location of the mites vary from person to person. One person could have twice as many as someone else. It's also possible to have them on one half of your face but not the other! But here is a bit of good news: The critters seem less likely to make themselves at home on kids' faces. So be sure to enjoy your last few mite-free years.

THE DISCOVERY WAS MADE DURING A 2014 STUDY THAT SEARCHED FOR FACE MITE DNA ON HUMAN SKIN. Previous studies had searched faces for only the critters themselves, sometimes by sticking a piece of tape on participants' skin and then peeling it off for inspection. Chillingly, the scientists behind the recent study describe the face mites as "arguably the animals with which we have the most intimate interactions."

REAL

HONEST
ABE

In the human body, there are ten times as many cells belonging to teeny-tiny **BACTERIA AND OTHER MICROBES** as human cells.

ANIMALS THAT MAKE HUMANS THEIR HOME

Like it or not, other critters live on—and in—you.
Can you guess which of the following
are REAL HUMAN INHABITANTS?

ROACH

THREADSNAKE

MICRO-CHAMELEON

TARDIGRADE

PINWORM

BEETLE

LOUSE

BUMBLEBEE BAT

ANSWER: Relax! The only animals on this list that live on humans are lice and pinworms.

21

ARTIST CREATES
INVISIBLE ARTWORK

Would you buy a piece of art that you couldn't see— ever—because it doesn't actually exist? Artist Lana Newstrom caused a stir when she put her invisible artwork on display at a New York City gallery and then invited people to come inside to "see" it. So that people would know where to look, she placed labels on the wall above where a piece of art was … or would be, if it were real. When people expressed trouble seeing anything other than a blank wall, Newstrom encouraged them to use their imagination, and then explained to them what the invisible art looked like in her mind. At the end of the evening, she invited her guests to enjoy one of the invisible beverages she'd provided.

FUN FACT

This particular story may be fake, but the Hayward Gallery in London, England, actually DISPLAYED INVISIBLE ARTWORK for two months in 2012.

THE ARTIST LANA NEWSTROM IS ABOUT AS REAL AS HER ARTWORK: The character was made up for a silly segment on the Canadian radio show *This Is That* in 2014. But some people who got wind of the story believed it was real, and it spread across the Internet. Perhaps they were fooled by a photo on the show's website of a crowd of people looking at bare walls. In reality, the image had been photoshopped to strip away the real artwork hanging on the walls of a gallery in Milan, Italy, in 2010. The pranksters also created a Twitter account and a professional website for Newstrom for added believability.

BIG OL' WHOPPER

WEIRD
HEAD GAMES

REAL OR FAKE?

Here's a sport where players really use their heads: **headis.** Just a few years old, the increasingly popular sport is a combination of Ping-Pong and soccer. Players stand at a Ping-Pong table and use their heads—and only their heads—to hit a seven-inch (18-cm) rubber ball back and forth. The founder of the sport says the idea came to him when he and his buddies wanted to play soccer, but the fields were always occupied. Ping-Pong tables, however, were often empty. He borrowed a child's ball, introduced the game to friends, and the rest is history! Headis may sound hilarious, but participants are serious about it: It's now part of the sports program at more than a dozen universities in Germany, where the game was first played. And it even has its own annual world championship!

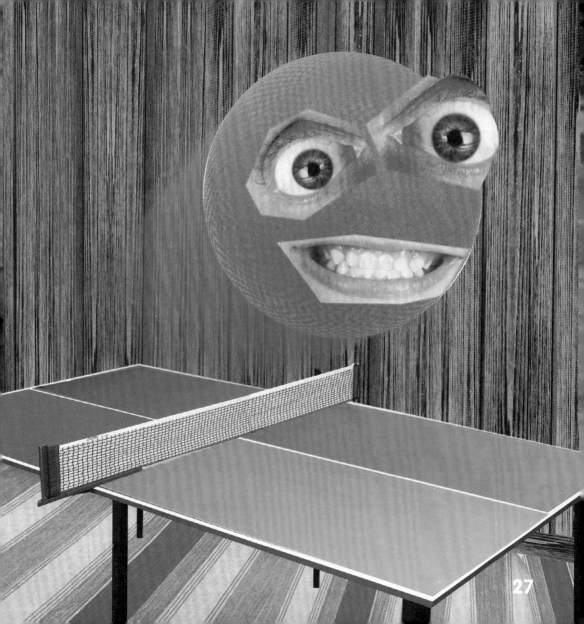

REAL

HONEST ABE

HEADIS IS JUST THE LATEST IN A LONG LINE OF WEIRD HYBRID SPORTS: Segway

polo, chess boxing, and unicycle jousting, anyone? Headis players have made the game even wackier by adopting funny names like Lord Voldehead, Armaheaddon, One Head Wonder, and Nosegrinder. Even more odd? Unlike Ping-Pong, you're allowed to jump up on the table to "spike" the ball.

29

WHY SLOTHS ARE SO SLOW

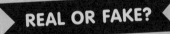

REAL OR FAKE?

Sloths—odd-looking and slow-moving—are strange creatures. But the reason behind their sluggish behavior may be even stranger. Curiously, sloths are extremely fearful creatures. Scientists studying the animals in the 1970s discovered that their heartbeat skyrockets at the sight or sound of harmless things that other animals seem to take in stride. For example, when exposed to the color yellow or the sound of crickets, sloths' heartbeats spiked from 22 beats per minute to over 100 beats per minute on average. Scientists speculate that because the animals are so easily spooked, they take a cautious approach to life, preferring to move very little and very slowly.

FUN FACT

Sloths travel, on average, only about 123 feet (37 m) a day. That's about one-third the LENGTH OF A SOCCER FIELD.

32

FAKE!

LITTLE
WHITE LIE

NO STUDIES HAVE SHOWN THAT SLOTHS SUFFER FROM A SLEW OF SILLY FEARS, SUCH AS CHIRPING CRICKETS OR YELLOW THINGS. Sloths have a very slow metabolism, which means that it takes their bodies a relatively long time to complete chemical processes, such as breaking down food. The animals remain still for long periods of time and otherwise move very slowly, and scientists think this behavior—combined with the camouflaging algae that grow on their coats—helps draw less attention from predators.

33

IDENTIFY THE LIE!

For each question group below, two statements are TRUE, and one is FALSE. Can you put your finger on the fib?

1

A. Ancient Romans used urine as mouthwash.

B. Tiger cubs are born furless and without any stripes.

C. Tiny critters called book scorpions live in the pages of old books.

34

2

A. You can mail a coconut without packaging it.

B. A flock of ravens is called an unkindness.

C. A pizza topped with flamingo and dormouse was found buried with Julius Caesar.

1. B: Tiger cubs are born fluffy little fur balls that already have their stripes, except in very rare cases. It is believed that one percent of tigers don't have stripes (but they still have fur!). 2. C: While flamingo and dormouse were commonly eaten by Roman nobles, there is no such pizza buried with Julius Caesar. In fact, Caesar was cremated, not buried, so there is no actual tomb or grave, simply a memorial site.

35

ANCIENT ROMANS
LAUGHED 'TIL THEY DIED

REAL OR FAKE?

If you could time-travel to ancient Rome to tell a joke, your **punch line would probably fall flat.** It may sound funny, but ancient Romans weren't allowed to laugh! For centuries, experts noted that no artifacts were ever found that depicted the Romans laughing. In 1931, suspicions of a no-laughing culture were confirmed when a team of archaeologists in Italy unearthed a tablet detailing a first-century B.C. Roman emperor's decrees. Rule number XXVI clearly states that laughing is an insult to the gods and an offense punishable by death. Historians speculate that in private homes, people likely did laugh. The urge to laugh, after all, is older than ancient Rome. And there was one place where laughing wasn't illegal: at publicly performed plays that were comedies.

FAKE!

LITTLE WHITE LIE

FUN FACT

Philogelos, often called the world's oldest surviving joke book, dates to the fourth or fifth century and contains 265 jokes. While some of its subjects are outdated, others—such as PASSING GAS AND BAD BREATH—are timeless.

38

ANCIENT ROMANS DID INDEED LAUGH. There's even a book about what they found funny: *Laughter in Ancient Rome,* by University of Cambridge professor Mary Beard. Interestingly, though, there is no word for "smile" in Latin, the language of the ancient Romans. Some historians have suggested that this points to a non-smiling culture, or at least one in which smiles were used differently in social situations than they are today.

VALENTINES
BUG OUT

This Valentine's Day, consider sending that special someone something hisss-terical: a hissing cockroach. For $25, Vindictive Valentines will mail someone a live hissing cockroach. For $5 more, the roach will be given the name of your choice. The company claims to have mailed more than one million cockroaches in its first year in business. To help meet demand, it's considering offering customers a second species. Visitors to the company's website can vote on whether that additional insect should be a dung beetle or a maggot. According to the owner of the company, the vindictive valentines are so successful because they hit home with everyone. "If you think about it, just about every person has someone in their past that they'd like to get even with. By mailing them a hissing cockroach, you can let them know exactly how you feel without having to talk to them," she said.

FUN FACT

Madagascar hissing cockroaches make their namesake sound by **FORCING AIR THROUGH BREATHING HOLES** on their abdomen.

FAKE!

BIG OL' WHOPPER

YOU DON'T HAVE TO WORRY ABOUT RECEIVING A HISSING COCKROACH IN THE MAIL. In 2015, though, the San Francisco Zoo did have a fund-raising campaign in which people could "adopt" hissing cockroaches and hairy scorpions in the name of their exes for Valentine's Day. Proceeds benefited the zoo and its animals (which stayed put).

WONDER WOMAN'S
WACKY HISTORY REVEALED!

REAL OR FAKE?

Most comic book heroes have epic origin stories: Think **Superman crash-landing on Earth.** But sometimes the story behind the creation of those characters is even more out of this world. Wonder Woman, a superhero whose magic lasso forces people to tell the truth, was created by the inventor of the lie-detector test! William Marston, a famous psychologist, was inspired by his studies on lying and by the women's rights movement of the early 20th century. His Wonder Woman stories stemmed from tales of Amazons in Greek mythology—female warriors who were strong and powerful. Wonder Woman is even depicted wearing Amazonian bracelets on her wrists. Marston not only created Wonder Woman, he also wrote the comics featuring her for seven years.

REAL

IT'S NO LIE: MARSTON, WHO PENNED THE WONDER WOMAN COMICS FROM 1941 TO 1947, INVENTED AN EARLY VERSION OF THE LIE DETECTOR USED TODAY.

In the comics, Wonder Woman has another cool gadget: an invisible plane. But so far, there's no evidence to suggest that it, too, was inspired by a real-life device.

SUPERHEROES

With their PECULIAR POWERS, superheroes can't help but stand out among ordinary humans. Can you GUESS which of the following have actually APPEARED IN COMICS?

MIND-SHAKE MAN: CAN CAUSE HIS ENEMIES' BRAINS TO MOVE BACK AND FORTH, CONFUSING THEM

ARMADILLO: CAN USE HIS TOUGH, ARMOR-LIKE SKIN TO WITHSTAND WEAPONS, FIRE, ICE, AND ACID

UMBRELLA WOMAN: CAN CONTORT HER BODY INTO AN INVINCIBLE UMBRELLA

KING ORANGE FREEZE:
CAN TURN ANYTHING ORANGE AND FROZEN IN AN INSTANT

DOCTOR STRANGE:
CAN BRING INANIMATE OBJECTS, SUCH AS ROCKS AND SHOES, TO LIFE

MATTER-EATER LAD:
CAN EAT ANYTHING

SQUIRREL GIRL:
CAN COMMUNICATE WITH SQUIRRELS AND HAS SMALL CLAWS AND A TAIL THAT CAN GRASP ALMOST ANYTHING

DAZZLER:
CAN TURN MUSIC INTO COLOR

ANSWERS: Armadillo, Doctor Strange, Matter-Eater Lad, Squirrel Girl, and Dazzler have all appeared in comics.

MAYOR PENS
PECULIAR POEM

Seattle, Washington, U.S.A., is a city where people do things a little differently. Still, citizens were shocked when the city's mayor released an official proclamation about a stinking flower, in rhyming verse and with made-up words. Mayor Ed Murray published his bizarre poem in celebration of Corpse Flower Week, dedicated to the plant whose bloom reeks of rotting meat. How weird was the poem? Here are a few lines to give you an idea: "Here in Seattle, we have one just now, and it seems as magical as a Beegiggle-wom-pow;" and "Flowers can be stinky, but parks make us merry, so let us now dance like a jiggle-wump berry."

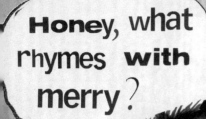

REAL

THE MAYOR OF SEATTLE REALLY DID RELEASE A WEIRD POEM ABOUT A FUNKY FLOWER IN 2014. And that's not the only time his wacky ways made headlines that year. While the U.S. president pardoned a turkey for Thanksgiving, per tradition, Murray instead pardoned a Tofurky, a turkey made of tofu, which was then donated to a food bank.

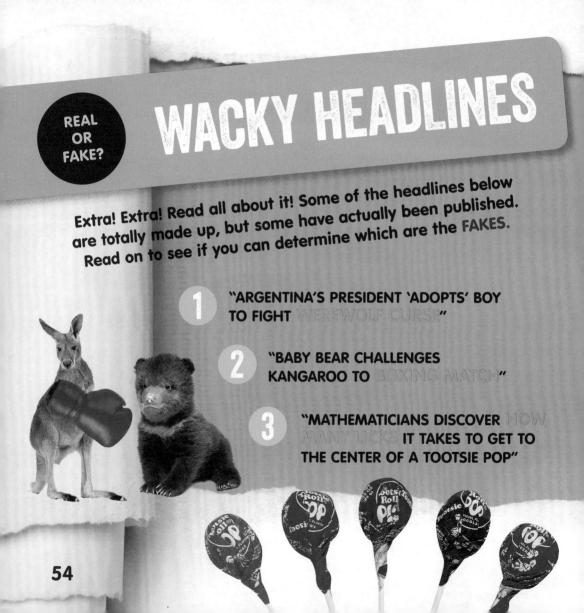

WACKY HEADLINES

Extra! Extra! Read all about it! Some of the headlines below are totally made up, but some have actually been published. Read on to see if you can determine which are the FAKES.

1 "ARGENTINA'S PRESIDENT 'ADOPTS' BOY TO FIGHT WEREWOLF CURSE"

2 "BABY BEAR CHALLENGES KANGAROO TO BOXING MATCH"

3 "MATHEMATICIANS DISCOVER HOW MANY LICKS IT TAKES TO GET TO THE CENTER OF A TOOTSIE POP"

4 "ONE-EYED ROCKFISH GETS A NEW GLASS EYE"

5 "100 BRAINS GO MISSING FROM UNIVERSITY"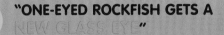

6 "MAN WAKES UP FROM COMA CONVINCED THAT HE'S MATTHEW MCCONAUGHEY"

7 "SNAPPING TURTLES SNAP SELFIES WITH iPHONE DROPPED INTO ZOO POND"

8 "BICYCLE BUILT FROM BANANAS COMPLETES CROSS-COUNTRY TREK"

9 "AUSTRALIA'S OLDEST MAN KNITS TINY SWEATERS FOR PENGUINS INJURED IN OIL SPILLS"

10 "WOMAN WHO WENT 15 YEARS WITHOUT BRUSHING HER HAIR FINDS WASP NEST IN IT"

ANSWERS: 2, 7, 8, and 10 are fake.

CLEOPATRA'S
SECRET COMMUNICATIONS

REAL OR FAKE?

It's well known that Cleopatra, ruler of ancient Egypt, lived an extraordinary life. What's less well known is that artifacts found in her tomb suggest that she had conversations with what some people believe were other-worldly beings. The so-called Cleo Papers, penned on papyrus, detail more than a dozen visits Cleopatra claims to have had with "exceptionally smart, tall, and long-limbed travelers." During one visit, the travelers told her about creatures that could be dinosaurs ("great lizard-like beasts once roamed not only Egypt but the whole planet," she wrote). During another, they gave her blueprints to build "a vessel suitable for travel to the stars." When she showed the sketches to the greatest mathematicians and engineers in her empire, she said, "they scoffed and said it could not be done." The blueprints, which could shed some light on just how advanced the travelers were, unfortunately have never been found.

FUN FACT

An ancient EGYPTIAN RECIPE FOR TOOTHPASTE calls for crushed rock salt, mint, pepper, and dried iris flower mixed together.

FAKE!

BIG OL' WHOPPER

THERE ARE NO PAPERS OF CLEOPATRA'S CLAIMING THAT SHE HAD CONVERSATIONS WITH MYSTERIOUS TRAVELERS TO HER EMPIRE. But there is a long history of associating aliens with ancient Egypt. Some people believe it's impossible that humans built the pyramids, despite evidence that shows how Earthlings could have accomplished the feat.

SIX DAYS
WITHOUT SUN

REAL OR FAKE?

This coming December will be very dark and very weird—for everyone on Earth, not just those north of the Arctic Circle. NASA has confirmed there will be six days of total darkness during the month. The news has spread across social media, with alarmed Earthlings curious to know the cause of the blackout. The culprit: "a solar storm, which will cause dust and space debris to become plentiful and thus block 90% sunlight." A solar storm of this magnitude has not occurred in the last 250 years, according to one website. So how can you prepare for six days (or 144 hours to be exact) of total darkness? Experts say to be sure to have flashlights and extra batteries on hand, and to get out in the sun before and afterward as much as you can.

ON VACATION

61

FAKE!

LITTLE
WHITE LIE

WOULD YOU TRUST SUCH EARTH-SHATTERING NEWS FROM A REPORTER NAMED "WARLOCK"?

That's the author of the original news story about the blackout, which appeared on a website in the fall of 2014. Though the site claims that NASA confirmed the news, a quick check of the space agency's website shows nothing of the sort. Meanwhile, further research into the website that originated the hoax reveals this statement: "[the website] is a combination of urban news and satirical entertainment to keep its visitors in a state of disbelief." "Satirical" means using humor to show the foolishness of something. Looks like all those who were fooled need to consider their news source next time.

SPOT THE FAKE!

Do you have the eye of a spy? See if you can tell which of these photos are REAL and which are really FAKE!

Somebody call in the demolition team! This wallflower is in a really tight spot!

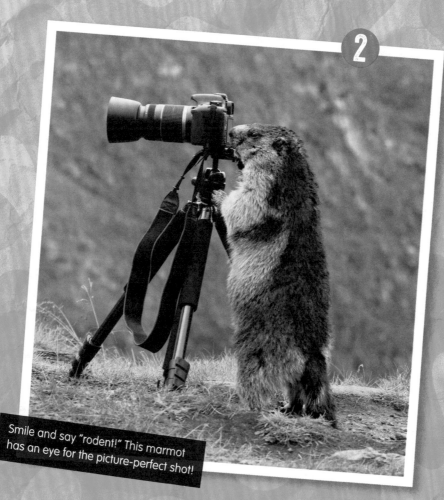

Smile and say "rodent!" This marmot has an eye for the picture-perfect shot!

SPOT THE FAKE!

1

Better buckle up—this art installation in London will leave you standing on your head!

You might have heard of the frog prince—but this one is king!

67

A butterfly finds the—uh—perfect perch in Everglades National Park, Florida, U.S.A.

Move over King Kong, there's a new towering terror in town.

IDENTIFY THE LIE!

For each question group below, two statements are TRUE, and one is FALSE. Can you put your finger on the fib?

1

A. "Plankter" is the singular of "plankton."

B. The oldest species of frog lands on its belly, not its feet, after it hops.

C. Mickey Mouse was originally named Ralphie the Rat.

2

A. Blue whale calves gain up to 50 pounds (22.7 kg) a day.

B. A camel can drink 500 cups (118 L) of water in ten minutes.

C. Buzz Aldrin was the first man to pee on the moon.

ANSWERS: 1. C: Mickey has always been named Mickey since his creation by Walt Disney in 1928. He was, however, created to replace his lesser-known predecessor, Oswald the Lucky Rabbit. 2. A: Blue whale calves actually gain up to 200 pounds (90.7 kg) a day! Considering they already weigh about 6,000 pounds (2,700 kg) at birth—that's one big baby!

HELLO ... HUMAN?

REAL OR FAKE?

Hello Kitty fans were shocked when Sanrio, the company that owns the cute character's likeness, announced that it needed to clear something up: Hello Kitty is not a cat. Never mind the name—or the character's feline face, for that matter. Hello Kitty is, the company said, instead cat-like. Reporters and fans then begged the company to explain what kind of creature Hello Kitty actually is. Some efforts only further confused things. A company spokesman offered this answer to one reporter who asked whether Hello Kitty, if not a cat, was a human girl: "It's difficult to provide a specific classification of what she is, or say something definitely, since everything is set in a world of characters." A visit to the Hello Kitty website, however, reveals this: "Hello Kitty is a cheerful and happy little girl with a heart of gold."

REAL

SANRIO CAUSED A COLLECTIVE HEAD-SCRATCH IN 2014 when it announced that the decades-old beloved character was in fact not a cat. It turns out there are many other interesting and largely unknown facts about Hello Kitty: Her real name is Kitty White; her hobbies include baking cookies and making pancakes; her blood type is A; she was born in the suburbs of London, England; and she has a twin sister, Mimmy White.

FUN FACT

Hello Kitty owns
a pet cat named
CHARMMY KITTY.

75

CHIMP CLIMBS
THE CHARTS

Pop superstars should watch their backs: There's a guitar-playing chimp whose acoustic song "Bananas" climbed to number 19 on music charts in Europe. It's no number-one record, but it's the most popular song ever performed by a nonhuman animal, Chester the chimp. Though Chester's owner crafted the song, the chimp learned how to play it after only two months of practice. When Chester strummed the correct note on the guitar, he was rewarded with his favorite treat, freeze-dried banana chips. Pretty soon, the chimp memorized the sequence. A recording of the tune made its way onto a radio station in 2012, and the rest is music history. The four-minute song has no lyrics, just Chester's grunts and shrieks throughout. But that hasn't stopped people from going—yep—bananas over it!

FAKE!

BIG OL'
WHOPPER

CHIMPS CAN PERFORM MANY IMPRESSIVE MENTAL AND PHYSICAL FEATS. But learning to strum an entire song on a guitar isn't one of them. Compared to humans, chimps' fine motor control isn't as developed, which means that they have a harder time doing delicate, precise tasks with their fingers.

PLANTS
MAKE MUSIC

REAL OR FAKE?

It may sound crazy, but plants can play tunes. A new device converts electrical currents moving across a plant's surface into synthesizer sound in real time. (Though the sound of the converted currents may not be music to your ears.) The device works in much the same way a lie-detector test does, only the probes are placed on leaves instead of on skin and the currents are translated into audio. What does this "music" tell us about the secret life of plants? The inventors aren't quite sure yet. They are, however, hoping the "biofeedback" will eventually be revealing, and help us learn more about the natural world. In the meantime, rest easy knowing that one day soon your houseplants could play a tune: An online fund-raising campaign to make the device available to people interested in purchasing it has reached its goal.

REAL

WITH ITS FAR-OUT SOUNDS, THE MIDI SPROUT ("MIDI" STANDS FOR "MUSI-CAL INSTRUMENT DIGITAL INTERFACE")

is changing the way people perceive plants. Scientists have known that plants send chemical and light signals to one another. Plants can even send chemical distress signals to get insects to come to their rescue! A study published in 2012 suggests that plants also may be able to use sound to communicate with one another, so why not talk to their human caretakers?

FUN FACT

The MIDI Sprout can even be HOOKED UP TO HUMANS! The electrical signals humans give off reportedly tell a lot about emotional states.

INVENTIONS

They say necessity is the mother of invention, but it's hard to believe people saw a need for these crazy creations! Check out the products below and decide which of these wild wares are REAL, and which are just the figment of a WILD imagination.

1 PERSONAL COMPUTER FOR DOGS

2 PORTABLE, PERSONAL RAINDROP COUNTER

3

A MACHINE THAT ANALYZES FINGERNAIL CLIPPINGS TO DETERMINE WHETHER SOMEONE IS A VAMPIRE

5

A BRUSH THAT ALLOWS YOU TO COMB YOUR HAIR AND TAKE "SELFIES"

6

DIAPERS FOR CHICKENS

4

A BLANKET THAT HUGS YOU

GHOSTLY GIRL
CAUGHT ON CAM

REAL OR FAKE?

A hunter who set up a camera to record nighttime deer movements got more than he expected when he checked his footage. Peering out of the darkness was not only a buck but also a ghostly-looking little girl in a gingham dress. The creepy photo circulated online, along with other reports of ghostly children captured on hidden hunting cameras. The images caused quite a stir and a number of questions. If the child was human and not a ghost, why didn't the deer run away? Readers wondered whether it was the same little girl or several different ghouls haunting hunting spots. Is there a not-so-camera-shy ghost in our midst?

LITTLE
WHITE LIE

FAKE!

THE SPOOKY PHOTO OF THE GHOST IN THE GINGHAM DRESS STARTED MAKING THE ROUNDS ON THE INTERNET IN 2011.

It turns out that the image was created with a smartphone app called Ghost Capture. It works by allowing users to snap a pic and then add one of 40 ghostly images! Another photo of a ghostly little girl, this time standing among two bucks, appeared online in 2014 but was revealed to be the work of a professional photographer; someone had posted it as a prank.

INSECT LIVES
IN SHEEP SNOT

REAL OR FAKE?

t's hard to find something nice to say about sheep nose bot flies. Soon after one hatches, its mother deposits it inside the nostrils of a sheep. The baby bot fly—which doesn't yet look like a fly; it's a worm-like maggot—wriggles its way up into the sheep's sinus cavities. There it settles in and munches on mucus for as many as ten months. Eventually it wriggles its way back into the sheep's nose, causing discomfort. The sheep, ready to shed its uninvited guest, which grows to a plump 1.2 inches (3 cm), has a simple way of getting rid of it: with a sneeze! Shot to the ground, the insect digs down and spends a few weeks turning into its adult, or fly, form, before busting loose and buzzing off to start the creepy cycle all over again.

FUN FACT

Bot flies can infiltrate people through the bite of a mosquito or tick and STICK AROUND FOR A MONTH OR TWO before wriggling their way out. While inside, the bot fly breathes through a pair of tubes attached to its rear, which poke out slightly from the person's skin.

REAL

HONEST ABE

BOT FLIES MAY BE ONE OF THE LEAST LIKABLE CREATURES IN THE WORLD. Different species infest not only sheep but also goats, horses, donkeys, cattle, and even people! Sheep try to keep bot flies out of their noses by sticking their snouts in the ground, shaking their heads, and sneezing.

BULLETPROOF
CANDIDATE

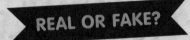

REAL OR FAKE?

The show must go on! In 1912, U.S. presidential candidate Teddy Roosevelt was preparing to give a campaign speech in Milwaukee, Wisconsin, when he was shot by a saloonkeeper named John Schrank. But instead of heading to the hospital, he insisted on being driven to the auditorium where he was scheduled to speak! There, he showed the crowd his bloodstained shirt and pulled out his bullet-hole-riddled, 50-page speech from his breast pocket. Incredibly, he went on to speak for more than an hour before he was finally rushed to the hospital. Fortunately, he lived to tell the tale—with the bullet lodged in a rib, where it remained the rest of his life.

Background text (partially visible, typed on paper):

-8-

...into politics thirty-two years ago... ...in...
...been that the only safe course t... ...ucky... neither dis...
...is to treat each man on his... ...neither dis...
...avor not against him because of his gree...
...Thirty-two years ago...
...ture, my close allie...
...ello, Costello and...
...had themselves been...
...Ireland or in Germ...
...considering wh...

AT FIRST, THE AUDIENCE HAD A HARD TIME BELIEVING THAT ROOSEVELT HAD REALLY BEEN SHOT. When one of his bodyguards attempted to explain what had happened, someone shouted, "Fake!" But the bloodstain and the bullet hole convinced the crowd. Roosevelt's first lines to the audience: "Friends, I shall ask you to be as quiet as possible. I don't know whether you fully understand that I have just been shot." Though Roosevelt's speech, folded in his breast pocket, very likely helped save his life, in the end it couldn't save his bid for the presidency: He lost.

REAL

whose parents had

neither they nor I were

irthplace of any one of us

of us professed or what la

All that any one of us dema

FUN FACT

Don't FEEL TOO BAD about Teddy's 1912 presidential loss. He had already served as U.S. president from 1901 to 1909.

ROBOT HITCHHIKES
ACROSS CANADA

REAL OR FAKE?

Would you give a talking, hitchhiking robot a ride? Nineteen carloads of Canadians did during the summer of 2014, helping the kid-size hitchBOT travel more than 3,700 miles (6,000 km) from Halifax, Nova Scotia, to Victoria, British Columbia. Anyone who offered hitchBOT a ride had to lift it into and out of the car—only its hitchhiking arm moves. But they were rewarded with a robot that can converse with its companions, including sharing facts about whatever region it's currently traveling through. The 'bot had a ton of fun along the way, sightseeing, making lots of new friends, riding a ferry, and attending a wedding and a First Nations powwow. It even captured all the action in photos, which it uploaded to its social media accounts!

HONEST
ABE

REAL

CANADIAN RESEARCHERS CREATED HITCHBOT TO STUDY HOW PEOPLE INTERACT WITH ROBOTS and to test technologies that allow the two to communicate. The robot, made from everyday household items but equipped with 3G mobile communications technology and GPS, has charmed people around the world, with recent travels including a tour across Germany in early 2015. Says hitchBOT's online bio: "Simply put, I am a free-spirited robot who wants to explore the world and meet new friends along the way."

RIA BC or BUST!

📱 www.hitchbot.me

FUN FACT

HitchBOT's sibling, KULTURBOT, travels too and tweets about art galleries.

IDENTIFY THE LIE!

For each question group below, two statements are TRUE, and one is FALSE. Can you put your finger on the fib?

1

A. Fireflies don't light up in the western United States.

B. "Hello" is the oldest word in modern human language.

C. Long ago, doctors used to taste a patient's urine to diagnose certain illnesses.

2

A. The indentation below your nose is called a philtrum.

B. The binturong, a Southeast Asian mammal, smells like buttered popcorn when excited.

C. On average, about five earthquakes occur worldwide each day.

ANSWERS: 1. B: Though the roots of modern English date back to the 5th century, "hello" is definitely not one of them. The word was popularized by Thomas Edison in 1877 with the invention of the telephone, as no one knew what to say when they answered. The term also won favor over the telephone inventor Alexander Graham Bell's preference, "ahoy." 2. C: Actually, thousands of tiny earthquakes happen every day.

103

DAREDEVIL FISHERMEN USE
FINGERS AS BAIT

REAL OR FAKE?

Would you stick your arm, all the way up to your elbow, into a big, live, wriggling fish's mouth? If you answered yes, then "noodling" might be right up your alley! The freaky fishing technique involves jamming your hands into murky, underwater nooks, risking injury from not only fish but also anything else that might be lurking there. Once they feel a fish, noodlers stick their bare hand and forearm into its mouth to haul it out. The fish, typically catfish, can be quite big: Heavyweights have tipped the scales at nearly 70 pounds (32 kg)! While the sport attracts a small following, it's popular enough that there's an annual tournament held every year in Oklahoma, U.S.A.

FUN FACT

Mekong giant catfish can reach ten feet (3 m) long and weigh 650 pounds (300 kg). NOW THAT'S A WHOPPER!

REAL

HONEST ABE

NOODLING HAS ATTRACTED AN INCREASING AMOUNT OF ATTENTION SINCE 2000, with competitors appearing in books, documentaries, and even several reality-TV shows. The annual Okie Noodling Tournament, in Pauls Valley, Oklahoma, has been held since 2001. Its slogan is "No hooks. No bait. No fear." And just in case you were wondering, yes, catfish have teeth.

APRIL FOOLS' DAY
STARTED BY JOKESTER

REAL OR FAKE?

There's a funny story behind the first April Fools' Day. The court jesters of Roman emperor Constantine I thought they could do a better job ruling than he could. So they asked the emperor to give one of them the chance to rule for a day. Incredibly, Constantine agreed to the silly substitute, and Kugel the jester was crowned for one day, April 1. From then on, Kugel declared, people would celebrate absurdity on that day. Today, hundreds of years later, pranks are pulled by thousands of people around the world on April Fools' Day, but few are aware of the holiday's origin. The story of Kugel wasn't published until 1983, in an Associated Press interview with Boston University history professor Joseph Boskin.

FAKE!

LITTLE
WHITE LIE

BOSKIN DID TELL THE STORY OF KUGEL TO THE AP REPORTER—BUT AS A PRANK! HE THOUGHT THE SILLY STORY WOULD SET OFF ALARM BELLS WITH THE REPORTER. He thought the name "Kugel"—a baked noodle pudding—would give it away. Explained Boskin in an interview with the Boston University newspaper: "Since I was calling New York, where kugel is famous, and it was April Fools' Day, I figured he would catch on. Instead, he asked how to spell 'kugel.'" So the story ran. Once the AP found out it was a prank, it published a correction.

FUN FACT

Though **KUGEL** is most often associated with noodles, it can also be made with potatoes.

111

ASTRONAUT INFESTATION
IS OUT OF THIS WORLD

REAL OR FAKE?

In what was dubbed the "out-of-this-world itch sitch" by the press, half the astronauts aboard the space shuttle *Triumph* were ordered to return to Earth after an epic outbreak of head lice struck the craft in 1994. At first, the astronauts took the outbreak in stride, making jokes while scratching their scalps during video conference calls with NASA. When things got worse, some shaved off their hair. But over time, the lice proved too powerful; the astronauts couldn't get rid of them. Worse, the crew members were becoming uncomfortable and distracted from their high-stakes duties. So they were sent home to recover. NASA says it's unsure how the lice boarded the ship, or if the extra-persistent pests were extraterrestrial.

FUN FACT

HEAD LICE CAN ONLY CRAWL;
THEY CAN'T HOP OR FLY. And
since they're each only .07 to
.11 inches (2 to 3 mm) long,
they can't travel far—unless
their human hosts do.

FAKE!

BIG OL' WHOPPER

ASTRONAUTS WERE NEVER SENT HOME BECAUSE OF *PEDICULUS HUMANUS CAPITIS*, THE DREADED HEAD LOUSE—OR ALIEN LICE, FOR THAT MATTER. Astronauts are trained to deal with minor medical problems. As long as they used medication to treat the lice and followed guidelines to get rid of them, the pests would eventually peter out. They can't live long without a human host.

MISSING LINK
FOUND

Scientists can stop searching for the so-called missing link in evolution—it's already been found. The long-looked-for species with characteristics of both apes and humans had been sought as proof of Charles Darwin's theory that humans evolved from apes. In 1912, amateur fossil hunter Charles Dawson brought skull fragments found in England to a scientist at the Natural History Museum in London, England, to study. The scientist, Arthur Smith Woodward, declared that they belonged to a new species that could be the missing link. It had an apelike jaw, humanlike teeth, and a brain case as big as a human's. Nicknamed the Piltdown Man, after the site where it was unearthed, the 500,000-year-old fossils were found mixed among stone tools and mastodon bones. Newspapers around the world put the discovery on the front page, and scientific history was made.

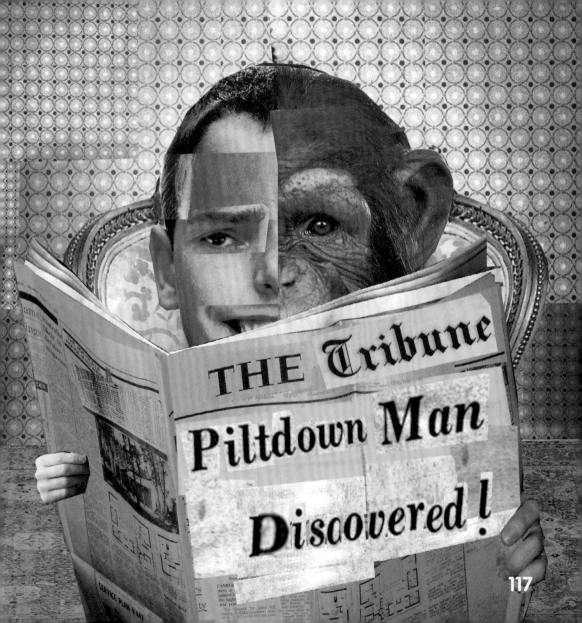

THE Tribune

Piltdown Man

Discovered !

FAKE!

THOUGH THE PILTDOWN MAN STORY IS RIPPED FROM THE HEADLINES, IN THE END, SCIENTISTS DISCOVERED THAT THE REMAINS WERE A SCAM. Experts grew increasingly suspicious of Piltdown Man as other early human skulls were found elsewhere that looked very different. And as technology improved, scientists could better inspect and date fossils. In 1953, it was announced that Piltdown Man was a hoax; the missing link was still missing. The fossil fragments of Piltdown Man's skull don't even belong to the same species, and some aren't even old. The jaw came from a modern ape— probably an orangutan—and chemicals were applied to it to make it look older. Scratches on the teeth suggest that they were filed down to look more like human teeth. And while the brain case was human, it wasn't nearly 500,000 years old.

FUN FACT

SO WHO WAS BEHIND THE PILTDOWN MAN HOAX? Charles Dawson, the man who discovered the fossil, is the prime suspect. But there are others, including Sir Arthur Conan Doyle, creator of the Sherlock Holmes series and an acquaintance of Dawson's.

TOWN GETS CUT OFF

The tiny town of Point Roberts, Washington, is in a peculiar position. The five-square-mile (13-sq-km) community lies at the southern tip of a Canadian peninsula but is actually part of the United States. Blame it on the 49th parallel, which the town sits just south of. This latitudinal line marks the boundary between Canada and the United States from Minnesota westward. The surveyors who mapped the border in the mid-1800s turned the town into an odd U.S. outpost when they refused to make an exception for the little piece of land and shift the border there just a few miles south. Consequently, because the town's residents are U.S. citizens, they must cross into Canada and then cross another border 25 miles (40 km) away back into the United States to do such everyday things as attend school, register for a driver's license, and go to the bank.

HONEST
ABE

REAL

Vancouver

Burnaby

Sea
Island

Richmond

Delta

Westham
Island

FUN FACT

The U.S. state of Alaska
is also an EXCLAVE.

CANADA
UNITED STATES

Point
Roberts

Galiano
Island

S A L I S H

POINT ROBERTS, WASHINGTON, IS WHAT'S KNOWN AS AN EXCLAVE OF THE UNITED STATES, or a territory that is physically separate from the rest of the nation and surrounded by another. Though the surveyors drew a hard line through the town, they didn't elsewhere: Just west of Point Roberts, the border was shifted south in order to include all of Vancouver Island within Canada.

Port Moody

B R I T I S H   C O L U M B I A

Surrey

Langley

Aberdeen

Boundary Bay

White Rock

CANADA
UNITED STATES

0   5 miles

0   5 kilometers

Blaine

S E A

W A S H I N G T O N

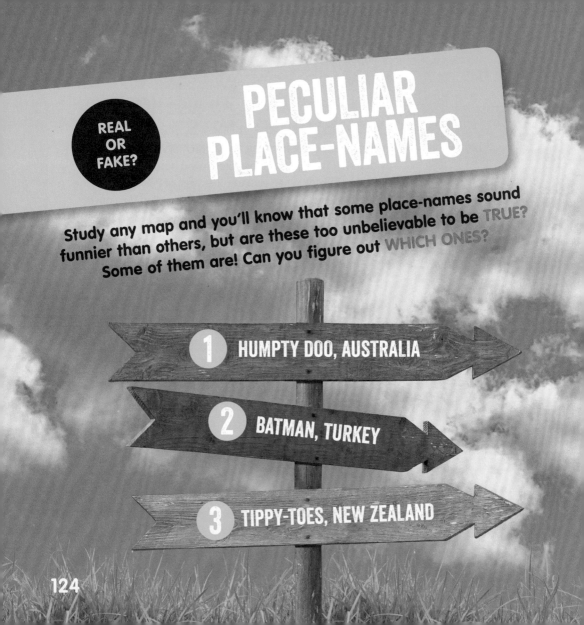

REAL OR FAKE?

PECULIAR PLACE-NAMES

Study any map and you'll know that some place-names sound funnier than others, but are these too unbelievable to be TRUE? Some of them are! Can you figure out WHICH ONES?

1 HUMPTY DOO, AUSTRALIA

2 BATMAN, TURKEY

3 TIPPY-TOES, NEW ZEALAND

4 CHEESEBURGER, WISCONSIN, U.S.A.

5 GEORGE, WASHINGTON, U.S.A.

6 CHICKEN SQUAWK, TANZANIA

7 ACCIDENT, MARYLAND, U.S.A.

8 MORE TOMORROW, BELIZE

9 SNOT, SCOTLAND, U.K.

125

ELEPHANTS USE FEET
TO TALK LONG-DISTANCE

REAL OR FAKE?

Sure, elephants use their big ears to hear. But did you know they can also "hear" through their feet and trunks? They do this by detecting vibrations that travel through the ground, sometimes over long distances. Scientists say elephants pick up the seismic sensations through bones in their toes. They've even been known to place one foot on tiptoe to better receive the signals, which travel from the toe bones to the ear. Special cells found on the tip of an elephant's trunk and the soles of its feet also help detect these disturbances in the Earth. Elephants are able to interpret what the vibrations mean—such as "it's raining" or "predator!"—and from which direction they're coming, even miles away! This comes in handy when they are trying to find water or avoid threatening animals, like lions.

REAL

HONEST
ABE

One of the ways you can tell an African elephant apart from an Asian elephant is by looking at the **TIP OF THEIR TRUNKS**. African elephants have a triangular structure on both the top and bottom of the tip. Asian elephants have this triangular structure only at the top. The structure acts like a finger, helping the animals grasp objects.

ELEPHANTS AREN'T THE ONLY ANIMALS THAT CAN COMMUNICATE THROUGH SEISMIC SIGNALS;

insects, spiders, and frogs, among others, do too! Scientists have observed that elephants will freeze when they detect the signals, presumably while they are processing the vibrations and deciding their next move. They'll also place their trunk on the ground and shift the position of their body to better pick up the signals.

BIZARRE BIRD
BAFFLES SCIENTISTS

REAL OR FAKE?

Scientists were left in disbelief after reading a report about a previously unknown bird species quite unlike any other. A published description of the species, based on a single skin brought back from New Zealand, listed several strange characteristics of the chicken-size creature. It has tiny, useless wings; no tail; hairlike feathers; and nostrils at the end, not the base, of its long bill. After reading the article and reviewing its illustrations, many scientists claimed the whole thing was a hoax—that the bird couldn't possibly be real. Instead, they insisted, the skin had been stitched together from several different birds. The bird is now a national symbol.

REAL

HONEST
ABE

WHAT YOU JUST READ IS THE STORY OF THE DISCOVERY OF THE KIWI BIRD

by a British Museum zoologist in the early 1800s. When the description was published in 1813, it caused a sensation. Over the years, enough evidence was eventually collected to convince those outside New Zealand that the kiwi was, in fact, real. And, it turns out, it's even weirder than originally believed. It was later discovered that kiwi eggs are hefty, weighing as much as one-fifth of the bird's body, and that kiwi bones are not hollow, unlike other birds'.

SPAGHETTI
GROWS ON TREES

REAL OR FAKE?

Money doesn't grow on trees ... but spaghetti does? The British Broadcasting Corporation blew thousands of minds after it aired a documentary about an annual spaghetti harvest on a picturesque family farm in Ticino, Switzerland. In it, women pluck spaghetti strands dangling from a tree and then lay them out to dry "in the warm Alpine sun." The narrator explains that the year's crop has been plentiful, thanks to a mild winter and the elimination of that dreaded pasta pest, the spaghetti weevil. Viewers also learn that each spaghetti strand grows to the same length, thanks to years of farmers figuring out which trees produce the right-size noodle. After watching the documentary, hundreds of people called the BBC to find out how they could acquire a spaghetti tree. Picking pasta from a tree would be so much easier than forming it by hand!

FAKE!

BIG OL' WHOPPER

HERE'S THE CATCH: THE DOCUMENTARY AIRED ON APRIL FOOLS' DAY IN 1957. It was a

joke. Spaghetti is typically made from wheat, a grass, but some viewers believed that pasta grew on trees. At the time, spaghetti was not widely eaten in the United Kingdom and was considered to be an exotic food. In response to viewers' questions about how to grow their own spaghetti tree, the BBC reportedly answered: "Place a sprig of spaghetti in a tin of tomato sauce and hope for the best."

FAMOUS STREET ARTIST ARRESTED—TRUE IDENTITY REVEALED

REAL OR FAKE?

t finally happened: Famed British graffiti artist Banksy was arrested. For more than a decade, Banksy has spray-painted his signature, beloved artwork on buildings around the world while managing to maintain a secret identity. And to rack up the bucks: He's reportedly worth an estimated $20 million! When he appeared on *Time* magazine's "100 Most Influential People in the World" list, he was photographed with a paper bag on his head. So it came as a shock to his fans when news spread that he had been apprehended by London, England, police and that his real name was Paul Horner. Prior to arrest, Banksy had gained so much notoriety that British police set up a 24-hour anti-graffiti task force to try to nab him.

POLICE DEPT

4 4 115 6-554

139

FAKE!

LITTLE WHITE LIE

FUN FACT

At a 2014 art auction at Sotheby's in London, Banksy pieces were reportedly PRICED AS HIGH AS $855,000.

BANKSY FANS BREATHED A SIGH OF RELIEF WHEN THEY EVENTUALLY FOUND OUT THE REPORT OF HIS ARREST WAS A HOAX. What gave it away? The story circulated in both 2013 and 2014, with slight changes in details, but each time it originated from websites known for publishing false stories. Paul Horner, however, is a real person who lives in Phoenix, Arizona. He is the perpetrator of the Banksy story and identifies himself as a serial hoaxer.

original Banksy art

ONE ODD JOB

Standing in line: Everyone hates it. Well, almost everyone. For a fee, one man will stand in line for you—for shoes, concert tickets, gadgets, food, you name it. He started standing in line for a living in 2012, and now his business is so popular that he has hired a team of line-sitters to help him out. His services are offered to people in the greater New York City area, and he charges $25 for the first hour and $10 for every half hour after that. He even delivers, too, in some cases: For $65, he'll wait in line on the weekend for two cronuts, the insanely popular New York City croissant-doughnut hybrid treat, and deliver them to your door. His business has grown so much that he's taken on employees—12 of them—who sit in an average of seven to ten lines a week. The company's motto? "Whatever you want, we'll wait for it."

FUN FACT

A 2009 poll of Britons found that the average adult spends 5 hours and 35 minutes waiting in line each month.

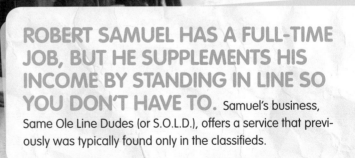

REAL

HONEST ABE

ROBERT SAMUEL HAS A FULL-TIME JOB, BUT HE SUPPLEMENTS HIS INCOME BY STANDING IN LINE SO YOU DON'T HAVE TO. Samuel's business, Same Ole Line Dudes (or S.O.L.D.), offers a service that previously was typically found only in the classifieds.

OTHER ODD JOBS

Some people do WEIRD THINGS for work.
Can you guess which of the following jobs are REAL?

HOTEL BED WARMER

SUBWAY TRAIN
PASSENGER STUFFER

PET FOOD TASTER

BAD BREATH
EVALUATOR

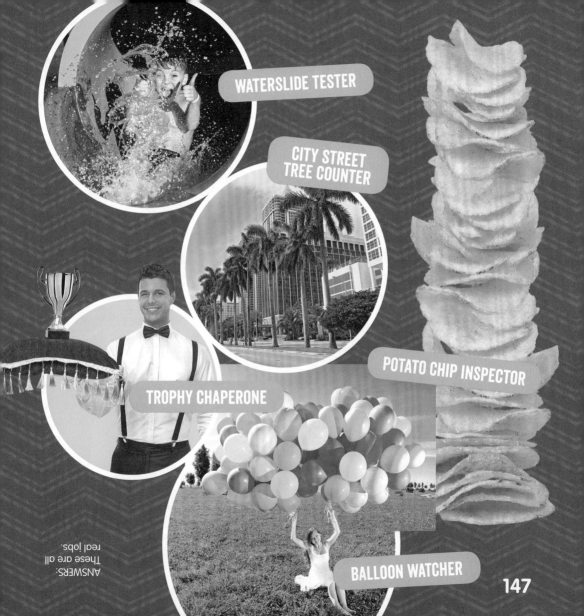

WATERSLIDE TESTER

CITY STREET TREE COUNTER

POTATO CHIP INSPECTOR

TROPHY CHAPERONE

BALLOON WATCHER

147

SPOT THE FAKE!

Do you have the eye of a spy? See if you can tell which of these photos are REAL and which are really FAKE!

1

Sharing your ice cream is one thing, but this gives a whole new meaning to the word "cowlick."

Who's upside down? Who's right-side up? This tricky pic will have you standing on your head.

SPOT THE FAKE!

1

A mermaid's bright orange fin stands out next to her dark gray dolphin pal.

150

Better watch your step! This deadly dino might make you his dinner.

GOBI'S
GIANT WORM

REAL OR FAKE?

In a popular 1990 movie, freakishly giant worms wriggled through rock and sand, terrorizing a small desert town. Amazingly, this may be art imitating life: In 1541, a caravan of traders traveling from the Middle East to Mongolia reported that they had battled and killed a giant, man-eating worm wriggling beneath the sands of the Gobi. The travelers' diaries recorded the chilling details: The creature was "longer than ten men laid end-to-end," as big around as "a great Cedar," and possessed of teeth "as long as a woman's forearm." The traders carefully packed the creature's skin to bring back home, but the harsh desert conditions turned it into brittle, crumbled bits. Few believed the travelers' tale upon their return. Their story would be completely forgotten were it not for one thing: the teeth, which did survive the journey, and have been on display at the British Museum since 1921.

FUN FACT

Explorer Roy Chapman Andrews, said to be the real-life inspiration for the Indiana Jones character, wrote about a mysterious, **WORMLIKE CREATURE RUMORED TO STALK THE GOBI** in his 1926 book, On the Trail of Ancient Man.

FAKE!

BIG OL' WHOPPER

THIS STORY WAS INSPIRED BY THE MYTHICAL, GIANT MONGOLIAN DEATH WORM OF THE GOBI. It's said to use electric shocks and burning acid to capture its prey. Unbelievably big and scary creatures such as the death worm are often rumored to live in vast, largely unpopulated places, where mystery and uncertainty can linger. But no hard evidence for this supersize worm has ever surfaced.

SPACECRAFT
LANDS ON COMET

REAL OR FAKE?

After traveling through the solar system for more than ten years and four billion miles (6.4 billion km), a spacecraft landed on a comet hurtling through space! For the lander, named Philae, the third time was the charm: It had bounced off the comet during its first two touchdown attempts, despite descending at the super-slow speed of two miles an hour (3.2 km/h). Sticking a landing was tricky because of the comet's low gravity, which is a hundred thousand times less than that on Earth. Philae seems to have landed on its side in a hole about 6 feet (2 m) wide and deep, and about 14 miles (22.5 km) from the comet's center. From this position, its onboard instruments have already sent back data—including close-up images of the comet's surface—for scientists to study.

REAL

HONEST
ABE

FUN FACT

The comet that Philae
landed on has BOULDERS,
BIG CLIFFS, AND PITS, as well
as JETS OF GAS AND DUST
bursting from the surface.

IT SOUNDS LIKE A FEAT FROM THE FUTURE, BUT SCIENTISTS ACTUALLY PULLED OFF THIS COMET LANDING ON NOVEMBER 12, 2014. The European Space Agency's Rosetta mission is the first accomplishment of its kind. Scientists didn't land a spacecraft on a comet just because it's cool, though. The craft has the important task of gathering information about "one of the oldest remnants of our solar system," said an agency official.

PAINT KEEPS
THE PEACE

In 1940, seven world leaders gathered in London, England, to decide which country would control the newly explored continent of Antarctica. After five days of fighting, an agreement was reached: Ownership of Antarctica would be divided up like a pie among the seven nations. But trust among the countries was lacking, and only worsened with the outbreak of World War II. So, in 1947, an international team was dispatched to paint bright blue lines across the ice that clearly marked each country's territory. It took 10 years, 36 sled-dog teams, and 67 surveyors and painters, but the task was well worth it: The lines still linger. The continent's extremely dry, cold conditions preserve the paint perfectly from the interior to about 85 miles (137 km) from the coast. Closer to the sea, the lines must be repainted periodically because of snowfall.

FAKE!

LITTLE WHITE LIE

FUN FACT

Antarctica has NO OFFICIAL TIME ZONE.

SEVEN COUNTRIES—ARGENTINA, AUSTRALIA, CHILE, FRANCE, NEW ZEALAND, NORWAY, AND THE UNITED KINGDOM have indeed made territorial claims to the Antarctic continent. The claims of Argentina, Chile, and the U.K. even overlap. But no lines were ever painted across the ice sheet, which today stretches about 5.4 million square miles (14 million sq km).

COUNTRIES BATTLE OVER
BIRD POOP

REAL OR FAKE?

Battles have been fought over many things: taxes, oil, spices ... poop? Control over Pacific Ocean islands covered in bird poop, or guano, led to a two-year battle between Peru and Spain during the 1860s. Why all the fuss over feces? At the time, guano was in high demand for use as a fertilizer. The dry climate of the Chincha Islands preserves poo from seafaring birds especially well. Giant piles of guano reportedly stood 150 feet (46 m) tall! Spain wanted to take control of the islands from Peru, a former colony. When they sent ships to the islands to scout, the Spanish people at first received a warm reception. Until one day a fight broke out between two Spaniards and a crowd of people. When the Peruvian government refused to apologize, it was the start of an all-out war. Peru prevailed, though, and to this day remains the rightful owner of the precious poo.

PERU AND SPAIN REALLY DID BRAWL OVER BIRD POOP. Guano is still harvested from Peruvian islands, though in far smaller amounts, which helps prevent the poo from disappearing forever. Heavy machinery is prohibited, with miners instead relying on pickaxes, shovels, and buckets for collection.

REAL

HONEST
ABE

NOW YOU CAN VISIT
SEAFLOOR CITY!

REAL OR FAKE?

In 2011, China stunned the world when it announced that it had secretly set up a city of 1,000 people on the seafloor off the country's southeastern coast. Encased in a giant, see-through dome, Seafloor City is protected from the surrounding waters by a 1,100-foot (335-m)-thick transparent material developed in a top-secret Shanghai lab. At two square miles (5 sq km), the city is small but packed with the nation's smartest scientists. The government has tasked them with studying an array of subjects, including marine life, simulations of human life on another planet, and how the human body might be able to adapt to life underwater. Seafloor City has now become a major tourist destination, even though you must be an expert diver to reach it. It was recently named National Geographic Traveler's top vacation destination of the year.

FAKE!

PEOPLE HAVE LONG DREAMED OF LIVING IN UNDERSEA CITIES, BUT NONE YET EXIST.

There is, however, an undersea research laboratory 60 feet (18 m) beneath the surface of the U.S. Florida Keys National Marine Sanctuary, in the Atlantic Ocean, where "aquanauts" can live and work underwater for weeks at a time. There are also a number of underwater hotels in the world that allow guests to actually "sleep with the fishes"!

IDENTIFY THE LIE!

For each question group below, two statements are **TRUE**, and one is **FALSE**. Can you put your finger on the fib?

1

A. Great white sharks are the deadliest animals on Earth.

B. Baskin-Robbins once made ketchup-flavored ice cream.

C. It's illegal to die in the town of Longyearbyen, Norway.

2

A. Former president Ronald Reagan loved beef jerky so much he kept a jar at his desk in the Oval Office and aboard Air Force One.

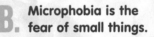

B. Microphobia is the fear of small things.

C. The stinky smell of blue cheese and sweaty feet is caused by the same bacteria.

ANSWERS: 1. A: Sharks are responsible for only about five human deaths worldwide each year. Mosquitoes, on the other hand, which are the deadliest animals on Earth, are responsible for thousands due to the diseases they spread. 2. A: Ronald Reagan did have a favorite snack that he kept nearby at all times, but it wasn't beef jerky—it was jelly beans. He loved them so much that the makers of Jelly Belly invented the blueberry flavor just so he could have red, white, and blue jelly beans at inauguration.

173

BIZARRE BURGER
BEGINNINGS

REAL OR FAKE?

A restaurant that claims to be the birthplace of the hamburger **has two rules that might surprise you:** No buns and no ketchup! No condiments at all, for that matter. Louis' Lunch, in New Haven, Connecticut, U.S.A., has been serving up hamburger patties on toast and topped with only cheese, onion, and tomato since 1900. The burgers have been made with the exact same ingredients on the exact same pans for more than 100 years! Despite the restaurant's limited menu (the only other food it serves are pie, potato salad, and chips), people have been lining up at Louis' for a long time. And its signature sandwich often lands on "best burger" lists, even though it's sans mayo, mustard, ketchup, and pickle. So the next time you make hamburgers at home, consider doing it the Louis way: Serve it on toast and keep the condiments in the fridge.

REAL

HONEST ABE

LOUIS' LUNCH SERVES BUN-LESS, CONDIMENT-LESS HAMBURGERS — AND HAS BEEN SERVING A LOT OF THEM FOR A LONG TIME. It's not the only restaurant with rules for its burgers, though: A Fort Myers, Florida, U.S.A., eatery forbids its waiters from serving ketchup or salt to diners over age ten. The chef says his burger already has a sauce on it, and there's no need to add anything.

LOUIS

UNCH

LOUIS

261-263

FUN FACT

Several other restaurants CLAIM TO BE THE BIRTHPLACE of the first hamburger, including Fletcher Davis, in Athens, Texas, U.S.A., in the late 1800s.

POPULAR FRUIT
FULL OF BUGS

Here's something to chew on: **There are little dead wasps littering the inside of figs.** Fig flowers are funny in that they grow in clusters concealed inside ball-like structures. A female fig wasp, drawn to the hidden flowers by a scent they emit, wriggles her way inside the ball to lay her eggs, then dies. After hatching, the wingless males perish inside, but not before digging an escape tunnel for the females, who then fly to other fig balls to lay their eggs. These balls become the fruit we eat— wasps and all. Yummy! The relationship between the wasps and the fig trees may seem weird, but it benefits them both. The wasps pollinate the figs, just as bees pollinate flowers. And the hidden flowers provide protection and food for young wasps and for those of us who eat them, well, everyone needs a little extra ... protein!

FUN FACT

Figgy pudding, best known for its appearance in the lyrics of a famous Christmas carol, IS ACTUALLY A FIG CAKE.

REAL

HONEST ABE

IF THE IDEA OF EATING ITTY-BITTY BUGS BOTHERS YOU, THERE'S GOOD NEWS: NOT ALL FIGS CONTAIN WASPS.

Some sold in stores are grown on trees that don't need pollinators to produce fruit. But if you really want to know whether wasps are in your figs, you can inspect the fruit closely. Or you can just eat the figs with insects—they're harmless.

MAN WALKS
ON WATER

REAL OR FAKE?

The United States Coast Guard had to burst one man's bubble after his attempt to walk on water through the Bermuda Triangle went awry. Encased in a large, inflatable bubble floating atop Atlantic Ocean waves, he planned to move it across the water by running—similar to how a hamster running in a wheel keeps it spinning. His bubble held a hammock that he planned to use to rest during the day when the sea was calm and temperatures topped 120°F (49°C). After training for years, he finally set sail from southeast Florida, and made it as far as 70 miles (113 km) off the coast of northeast Florida. Then the Coast Guard determined he was in danger and needed to be airlifted out. They were able to helicopter him to safety, but much to the man's dismay, the bubble had to be left behind. It's presumably still adrift at sea.

REAL

HONEST ABE

A MAN REALLY DID RUN ON WATER IN A GIANT BUBBLE IN 2014. The Coast Guard was called in after several concerning communications with the man, who initially refused a rescue; he was reluctant to end the run, which was for charity. He hopes to get his bubble back somehow, if it hasn't already deflated and sunk or been picked up by someone with a boat.

SPOT THE FAKE!

Do you have the eye of a spy? See if you can tell which of these photos are REAL and which are really FAKE!

1

This jumbo jumper might need a little help clearing this hurdle!

They say never open an umbrella indoors, but this occasion might be the exception.

2

The sky's the limit for German pianist Stefan Aaron, who plays while suspended from a helicopter.

1

Look out behind you! You never know when nature is going to sneak right up on you.

RHINO RAMBLES
ACROSS
COLLEGE CAMPUS

REAL OR FAKE?

Nearly a century ago, Cornell University students awoke to a curious sight on their Ithaca, New York, U.S.A., campus. In the snow were tracks from a very large animal that when followed led to a huge hole in a frozen lake. A professor of zoology summoned to help solve the plus-size puzzle gave a shocking identification: The footprints belonged to a rhinoceros. Baffled, people assumed the beast—escaped from where?—had fallen in and drowned. The incident then took another odd turn: The lake was the source of the university's drinking water, so some students and faculty swore off tap water. Those who continued to drink it claimed it tasted like rhino.

FAKE!

LITTLE WHITE LIE

TALK ABOUT A CLASS CLOWN: Hugh Troy, who attended Cornell in the 1920s and was a serial prankster, was reportedly behind the rhino footprints. The story—still told by students today—goes that while no rhino actually roamed the campus, a real rhino foot was in fact used to make the imprints. Troy found the foot, which had been hollowed out, and with the help of a friend used it to lay the tracks. Interestingly, some people claim the prank never actually happened—that Troy made up the tale later in life!

TORNADOES
CATCH FIRE

Sharknadoes—**vortices of snapping sea creatures that were the stars of a silly 2013 movie**—thankfully aren't real. But have you heard of firenadoes? The equally scary-sounding weather phenomenon forms when winds near a large fire whip flames and smoke into a vertical spin. They can reach heights of well over 100 feet (30 m). And their winds have been estimated to reach speeds of more than 100 miles an hour (161 km/h). These turning, burning towers don't just look terrifying. They're also dangerous, with the core reaching over 1000°F (538°C): In 1923, a firenado following an earthquake killed thousands of people in Japan. These twisters are one more reason to steer clear of a blaze that could spin out of control!

FUN FACT

MORE TORNADO TERMINOLOGY:
A dust devil is a swirling tower of, yep, dust, and a waterspout is a weak tornado that forms over water.

REAL

HONEST ABE

VIDEOS OF THESE VORTICES, ALSO CALLED FIRE WHIRLS, HAVE GONE VIRAL SEVERAL TIMES SINCE 2000.

While some viewers may ponder whether the swirling flames—filmed everywhere from the United States to Australia—are real, scientists have long known about firenadoes; however, they were only recently captured on film.

ARMCHAIR ADVENTURER
GOES AIRBORNE

Most hair-brained schemes never get off the ground. But one California man's did, literally, when he was lifted into the air for a 20-mile (32-km) flight while seated in an aluminum lawn chair buoyed by the weather balloons tied to it. He brought along only a few items: a parachute, a soda to sip on, a radio in case he needed to call for help, and a BB gun. When he flew so high that he started to grow numb, he simply shot a few balloons to drift to a lower altitude. But then he became entangled in a power line not far off the ground, so he hopped out, uninjured, and ended his 45-minute flight. But his fame had just begun. His airborne adventure made the news in the papers and on TV, and a movie was even made about it.

REAL

HONEST
ABE

"LAWN CHAIR LARRY" SET SAIL IN 1982 FROM A BACKYARD IN SAN PEDRO, CALIFORNIA, U.S.A., AND TOUCHED DOWN IN LONG BEACH.

Airline pilots reported seeing Larry soar at 16,000 feet (4,877 m)! Larry told a newspaper reporter that though the flight fulfilled a childhood fantasy of his, he had been lucky, adding, "You couldn't pay me a million dollars to do it again."

FUN FACT

The extreme sport of FLYING AROUND IN CONTRAPTIONS with large, helium-filled balloons tied to them is called cluster ballooning.

*Not actually Lawn Chair Larry

INDEX

Illustrations are indicated by **boldface.**